BYGONE PUBS OF DERBY AND DERBYSHIRE

BY ANTON RIPPON

north
bridge .co.uk
PUBLISHING

First published in Great Britain in 2014 by

North Bridge Publishing
20 Chain Lane
Mickleover
Derby DE3 9AJ

ISBN 978-0-99267-797-8

Book design by Graham Hales, Derby
Printed and bound by Mixam (UK), Watford
Vist the North Bridge Publishing *website for our other local books* www.northbridgepublishing.co.uk
or search on Amazon for North Bridge Publishing

"Pure and Wholesome Beverages"

"THE quality of ales and beers turned out is second to none, and the public demands for these pure and wholesome beverages have increased wonderfully. So Derby's brewing industry was described in 1891 when the town boasted four main breweries – Offiler's, Stretton's, Alton's and the Derby Brewery – as well as a number of – albeit steadily decreasing – small home-brewing houses.

For centuries the unique aroma of malt and hops hung heavily over Derby. In 1588 the town had one alehouse for every forty people; a century later the figure was one for every thirty-four townsfolk. As far back as the days of Henry III, almost 750 years ago, Derby was famous for its malt and ale. Indeed, until the Industrial Revolution malting and brewing were the town's main trades.

One of the four main breweries mentioned in 1891, Alton & Company, could trace its origins back to 1788. The Alton operation was in the Wardwick and a publication of the time described it as "a gigantic concern". Alton's, it was said, "is in the front rank of British brewers". In 1869, William Alton and Edward Barnett took over the original brewery started by Thomas Lowe. Alton eventually became the sole owner, later taking into partnership one George D'Arcy Clarke.

When William Alton died, his nephew, Hepworth T. Alton, took his place, and Arthur Walkden also joined the partnership.

Alton's, though, did not have long to live as an independent brewery. In 1903 it was taken over by Stretton's Derby Brewery, although brewing continued at the Wardwick until 1922 when the operation there was closed down and production moved to Stretton's Ashbourne Road premises.

Stretton's Manchester Brewery on Ashbourne Road was first mentioned in 1871. It was registered as Stretton's Derby Brewery in 1890; nine years later it took over the actual Derby Brewery that had been operating, in one form or another on Nottingham Road, since about 1830.

Derby Brewery had begun life as Robert Clarke & Son, assuming the Derby title in 1889. Again the praises of another local beer-making concern were highly sung according to the publication *Derby Illustrated*: "The Derby Brewery in Nottingham Road may fairly rank as one of the finest in the country ... The plant is of the most perfect character ... the most ingenious ideas have been put into practice." It also seems to have been something of a landmark: "The Derby Brewery presents a very imposing external appearance, the new chimney stack being conspicuous for miles around."

So Stretton's acquired the Derby Brewery, and also Alton's in keeping with its aspirations to control other breweries and, consequently, many more public houses. Between 1890 and 1895, Stretton's bought or leased many pubs in the Derby, Leicester and Potteries areas.

In 1893 there was a demand to aerate bottled beer instead of allowing it to mature in the bottle, for the clarity of the product was now all-important. Around that time Stretton's brewed a draught bitter, a best bitter and a dark mild.

It was the mild that proved most popular until, over the years, beer drinkers' tastes switched largely to bitter.

Stretton's, too, was to feel the wind of change. In 1927 the company was taken over by Samuel Allsopp & Sons, one of the largest brewery companies operating in Burton upon Trent. Brewing at Ashbourne Road ceased immediately, although the name of Stretton's was to live on until being slowly absorbed by Ind Coope Ltd, and then by Allied Breweries.

Offiler's began as the local brew of the Vine Inn, in Whittaker Street, Derby, in 1877 by George Offiler. In 1884 the brewery business moved from the pub to a former ordnance dept (hence nearby Depot Street) in Ambrose Street, off Normanton Road. After the ordnance depot had moved out, a firm of silk throwsters had used the building, and then it was used as a tea warehouse before Offiler's moved in.

Offiler's served most of the free houses in Derby. Workers started their shifts at 6am with a pint of beer, and they were each allowed four more pints during the course of the working day. Horses – which were stabled in Normanton Road – pulled the beer drays, while Offiler's sales representatives travelled the streets of Derby and beyond by horse and gig.

At the start of the First World War, Offiler's bought their first steam-powered lorries. Trade increased and a second brewery was opened at Cavendish Bridge to supply pubs in Leicestershire. One of Offiler's proudest moments came in 1946 when Derby County's FA Cup winning team travelled from the Blue Peter at Alvaston to Full Street aboard an Offiler's dray.

But the golden days of beer brewing in Derby were drawing to a close, for the time being at least. In 1965 Offiler's became a subsidiary of the huge Charrington United Breweries group, and on 30 September 1966 the last beer was brewed in Ambrose Street. The premises were still used as a distribution centre until 1968 when the last brewing connection with the old site ended. Charrington's was itself swallowed up by Bass, and the Offiler's identity went with it. For a time, a former Offiler's pub, the Crystal Palace in Rosehill Street, continued to brew. So, too, did the Exeter Arms until both pubs found it impractical to continue. The once renowned Derby ales were no more. A brewing tradition that had stretched back over centuries came to an end, beaten by the need for an economic operation.

Of course, in the 21st century, brewing is once again alive and well in Derby. If not on the giant scale of the 19th and early 20th centuries then certainly thriving and healthy with several companies and pubs brewing their own.

The purpose of this book, however, is show the way it was, using photographs of local pubs as they used to look. We hope that you enjoy them. Cheers!

Anton Rippon
Derby
2014

Bygone Pubs of Old Derby Town

The Alvaston Hotel on London Road, with an Ind Coope & Allsopp sign atop its roof.

(Right) The Babington Arms stood at the intersection of Babington Lane and Green Lane. It was demolished in 1928 to make way for the widening of Babington Lane after Derby Corporation bought it from the Nottingham Brewery Company for £5,000.

The Bedford Arms is one of many Derby pubs that takes it name from the street in which it is situated. This photograph dates from the 1950s.

The Bird Inn, tucked away where Jury Street met Willow Row opposite the lower end of Walker Lane, was demolished in 1912, another victim of street widening.

The Broadway Hotel was a private house latterly known as Darley Lodge before it became a pub in 1933.

(Left) The Blue Bell Inn, Upper South Street off Uttoxeter Old Road, was demolished in 1972.

The Brunswick Inn was designed by the Midland Railway's architect, Francis Thompson, to serve nearby railway workers' homes. It closed in 1960 but reopened in 1983 and started its own brewery in 1991.

The Chesterfield Arms that stood on Nottingham Road was a beerhouse only throughout its existence.

There had been a pub called the Coach and Horses on the corner of Mansfield Road and Old Chester Road since the early 18th century but in 1905 it was rebuilt in Edwardian style, complete with a bowling green.

(Left) The City Tavern at the corner of New Chester Street and Vivian Street pictured in 1911. By 1940 the pub's name had been changed, somewhat mysteriously, to the Garden City.

(Left) The Canal Tavern stood on Cockpit Hill from 1800 to 1972 when it made way for the Eagle Centre development.

The Crown Inn, Curzon Street, when it was run by Offiler's Brewery, who purchased it in 1913. The building was originally the residence for the manager of an adjacent malting and bakery business.

The Castle and Falcon stood on Cockpit Hill, at the corner of East Street, until it, too, gave way for the Eagle Centre development in 1972. Although no architectural gem itself, its modern replacement left much to be desired.

(Right) The Cavendish Hotel on the corner of Walbrook Road and Upper Dale Road dated from 1898. Soon after it was opened it was a rallying point for the departing Robin Hood Rifles foreign service detachment.

The Corporation Hotel was built in 1861 as part of Derby's new cattle market. It closed and was demolished in 1970. Among the many artists to have performed there in the early 1960s was a young Rod Stewart.

(Right) Ye Olde Dolphin Inn building in Queen Street dates from at least the mid-17th century, although the pub claims to have been existence from the mid 16th- century. Between 1927 and 1984 Offiler's owned it.

The Earl Grey stood on the opposite side of Upper South Street to the Blue Bell Inn (*qv*). Like the Blue Bell Inn it was demolished in 1972.

The Fox and Owl stood in Bridge Gate in the 1730s but was rebuilt in the 1880s to look like this. It was cleared, along with the rest of the area, in 1966/67.

The Green Dragon in St Peter's Street, near The Spot, was opened around the beginning of the 19th century. In the early 1930s it was refronted. It closed in December 1969 and was demolished soon afterwards.

(Left) The Grange Hotel stood in Malcolm Street, on its corner with Grange Street that was once the drive to Normanton Grange.

(Left) The Green Man Inn in St Peter's Churchyard originally stood in this 17th-century building. Offiler's were running it when it was gutted by fire in 1936. It was restored but had lost most of its original charm.

The Horse and Trumpet stood in Full Street from at least 1761 until 1939 when Offiler's inexplicably demolished it and replaced it with an uninteresting building that itself was closed in 1967.

The King's Arms County Hotel in St Mary's Gate dated from the late 17th century. After it closed in 1934 it saw service as a library and a divisional police station.

(Right) The King's Head in Cornmarket was one of Derby's classic coaching inns before it was closed in 1863 and demolished to accommodate the widening of St James's Street.

The Leopard in Grove Street, pictured here in the late 1930s, was a Stretton's pub that was closed in 1965 after being compulsorily purchased by Derby Borough Council.

The early-Victorian Litchurch Inn in Russell Street at its junction with Cotton Lane. It is pictured here in 1912.

The Lord Belper was a beer house that stood at the corner of Abbey Street with Spa Lane. It closed in 1959 and was eventually demolished. The site is still vacant.

The Norman Arms in Village Street was originally built by Stretton's in 1864 but was rebuilt on a slightly different site in the 1930s due to the extension of Kenilworth Avenue.

The 16th-century timber-framed Nottingham Castle stood on the corner of Queen Street and St Michael's Lane. It was closed in 1962 and demolished for no clear reason because the site remained empty for decades.

(Right) The Old Bell Hotel is another of Derby's classic coaching inns, functioning as such from the 1680s. It was originally a large brick-built inn but in 1929 it was given a half-timber refrontage. In 1988 Bass sold it to a property company and since then it has had a sad and chequered career before being rescued by an entrepreneur.

The Old Silk Mill in Full Street is known to have been operating since the 1870s. To accommodate Sowter Road (necessary for the Power Station) it was demolished in 1924 and rebuilt, on a slightly different site, in 1928. This photograph shows the inn just after the end of the First World War.

(Right) In 1876 the medieval Old White Horse made way for the new Friargate station of the Great Northern Railway. It was at one time home to Ellen Beare, the 18th-century abortionist and fraudster

The Old White Lion on Ashbourne Road, at the corner of Brick Street, was functioning as a beer house in the 1870s. It was then converted into a butcher's shop.

(Right) The Pear Tree Inn on St Thomas's Road, seen here in the late 1930s, replaced an earlier pub of the same name.

The Pelican stood on the corner of Abbey Street and Lower Stockbrook Street. It was open by 1857 and closed in 1979, shortly after which it was demolished.

The Plumber's Arms in East Street was demolished in 1885 to make way for new shops. In fact, the pub's address had been Bag Lane. The thoroughfare was changed to East Street shortly before the pub shut.

The Prince Regent stood in Regent Street, off Osmaston Road. It opened in the 1820s and closed in 1965 when the Derbyshire Royal Infirmary was extended.

(Right) The Queen's Head was sandwiched between Ranby's store in Victoria Street. An ancient inn dating from at least 1764, it closed in 1959 and was demolished in 1961 when the store was rebuilt.

The Roebuck Inn on the corner of Amy Street and Stockbrook Road, a late 19th-century pub that was demolished in the 21st century to make way for private dwellings. The war memorial commemorating those of its patrons who fell in the First World War was re-erected on the site.

(Right) The Seven Stars in King Street has long been one of Derby's best-known inns. It was here by 1775. Beer was once brewed on the premises.

The St Helen's Inn on Duffield Road pictured c.1890. It was completely rebuilt in the 1930s and is now renamed the Five Lamps.

Stretton's opened the Sinfin Hotel in 1934. Ansell's rebuilt it and reopened as the Cock 'n' Bull in 1982.

The Olde Spa Inn looks much the same today as it stands in Abbey Street, but now surrounded by industrial units rather than by the small terraced houses from where it drew its customers. Originally part of a spa complex opened in 1773, it was established as an inn in 1835 when Abbey Street was pitched. Until 1941, beer was brewed on the premises.

(Left) The Sir Frederick Roberts stood on the corner of Yates Street and Pear Tree Road. It was a beer house in the 1870s.

The Star and Garter in St Mary's Gate at the corner of Bold Lane. One of Derby's oldest pubs – it was described as such in the 19th century – it was closed in 1940 and later became transformed into offices for Derbyshire County Council.

The Station Inn on Midland Road, pictured here in the 1950s, was opened in the 1850s.

The White Bear Inn stood at 17-18 Derwent Row, on the corner of Exeter Street, near the Derby Canal, a lock of which was named after the pub. Opened in the 1820s, the pub closed in 1969.

The Vine Inn at the foot of Wilson Street was operating from the 1860s and closed in 1991. The Lifeboat, reputed to be Derby's smallest pub, is further up on the left. The Lifeboat closed in 1980 and was demolished in 1984.

The York Tavern in York Street is a small inn converted from a private dwelling and opened in the 1840s. It is one of the many Derby pubs that began life as a terraced house.

... and Some Bygone Pubs of Derbyshire

Burnaston: The Spread Eagle.

Belper: The New Inn *(right)*.

Belper: The White Swan.

Chaddesden: The Park Hotel.

Codnor: The New Inn.

Chellaston: The New Inn *(left)*.

Coxbench; The Fox and Owl.

Dale Abbey: The Stanhope Arms.

Findern: The Greyhound Inn.

Etwall: The Spread Eagle *(left)*.

Hartshorne: The Bull's Head.

Heanor: The Nag's Head *(right)*.

Heanor: The Ray's Arms, and The Old Jolly Colliers *(left)*.

Holbrook: The Cross Keys.

Holbrook: The Greyhound Inn.

Holbrook: The Spotted Cow.

Idridgehay: The Black Swan.

Ilkeston: The Bridge Inn, and The Brunswick Hotel *(right)*.

Ilkeston: The Middleton Hotel.

Kilburn: The Grand Turk *(right)*.

Marlpool: The White Lion.

Littleover: The White Swan *(left)*.

Melbourne: The Roebuck Inn.

Mickleover: The Great Northern (right).

Mickleover: The Vine Inn.

Milford: The William IV.

Ockbrook: The Cross Keys.

Ockbrook: The Queen's Head.

Ripley: The Rose and Crown, and The Cross Keys *(left)*.

Smalley: The Bell Inn.

Spondon: The Wilmot Arms *(right)*.

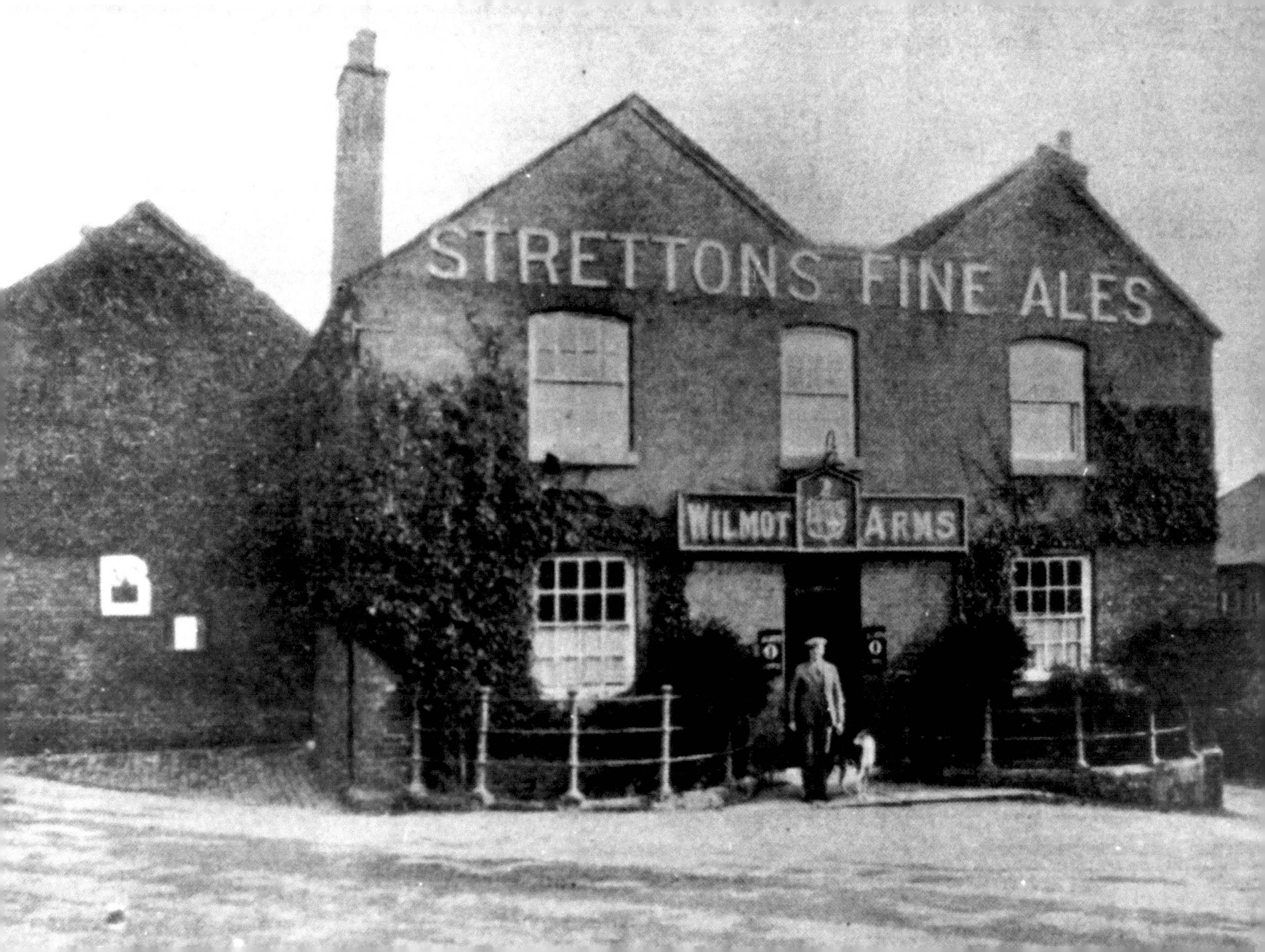
STRETTONS FINE ALES
WILMOT ARMS

Stanley: The Bridge Inn.

Turnditch: The Tiger Inn.

West Hallam: The Punch Bowl, and The White Hart *(left)*.

North Bridge Publishing produce a selection of local books on Derby.

Derby County: Story of A Football Club
Derby Memories
The Day That Derby Won The Cup
When The Rams Met The Nazis
It Happened in Mickleover
Derby: The Thirties and the War Years
Derby: The Fifties and Sixties

Please regularly visit our website or twitter page for new titles.